B♭ **Tenor Saxophone**

Warm-ups and Beyond

A Comprehensive Rehearsal Book for Developing Bands

BY TIMOTHY LOEST

with Percussion By Kevin Lepper

Table of Contents

Part 1 – Basic Warm-ups

This section of the book will take you through five major key signatures and their relative minors. Each relative minor key shares the same key signature with its related major key, but begins and ends on the note found a major sixth above (or minor third below) the tonic (home tone) pitch of the major key. For example, if the major key is C, the relative minor would be A minor.

You will rehearse these keys in the following format:

1. Major/Minor Fives (quarter notes) – This exercise moves up and down the first five notes of each scale, followed by an arpeggio (scale tones 1 – 3 – 5 – 3 – 1).

2. Major/Minor Fives (eighth notes) – This is the same exercise as No. 1 using eighth notes instead of quarter notes.

3. Thirds – Using the first five notes of the scale, this exercise will move up and down by thirds (moving by skip rather than by step).

4. Expanding Intervals – On the ascending part of this exercise, notes after the repeated tonic (home tone) grow in interval (space between notes). On the descending part of this exercise, the dominant tone (the fifth scale tone) is repeated as the descending notes grow in interval. Only the first five notes of the scale are used.

5. Percussion Feature.

6. Follow the Leader – This exercise uses the first five notes of the scale and moves by step. Soloists or sections play first and are then echoed by the band. Everyone plays in unison and octaves in the last two or four measures.

As always, read your parts carefully, and pay attention to all of the directions that the composers and your director give you. Watch your conductor as the dynamics and time signatures change. Breathe where the breath marks are indicated and maintain good breath support for a clear sound.

Basic Warm-ups Key Challenge

Playing by ear is an important skill for all performing musicians. Once you have gone through Part 1, you will really know the format well. Challenge yourself to try a few additional keys. You can do this by ear with the help of your director.

For example, select concert D♭ major or concert G major. Make the transposition for your instrument to figure out what your key will be. Review the flat or sharp notes that you will need and consult your fingering chart if necessary. Play the tonic or home tone, then sing up the first five notes of the scale (do - re - mi - fa - sol). Sing back down to the tonic note, then find the second note of the scale on your instrument. Continue in the same way until you have found all five notes. Once you have learned these new notes by ear, you will be ready to apply them to the exercises found in Part 1.

Concert C Major

1. Major Fives – Quarter Notes

2. Major Fives – Eighth Notes

3. Thirds

4. Expanding Intervals

5. Percussion Feature
Liftoff!

Listen and watch carefully as the percussion section plays.

6. Follow the Leader

BB203TSX

Concert A Minor

1. Minor Fives – Quarter Notes

scale   arpeggio

2. Minor Fives – Eighth Notes

scale   arpeggio

3. Thirds

4. Expanding Intervals

5. Percussion Feature

A Bumpy Ride Smooths Out

Listen and watch carefully as the percussion section plays.

6. Follow the Leader

solo/soli   band   solo/soli   band

solo/soli   band   all

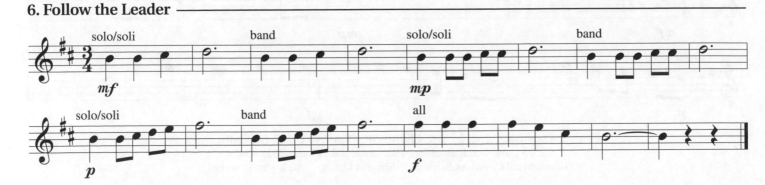

Concert F Major

1. Major Fives – Quarter Notes

2. Major Fives – Eighth Notes

3. Thirds

4. Expanding Intervals

5. Percussion Feature

The Control Lights Go On and Off!

Listen and watch carefully as the percussion section plays.

6. Follow the Leader

Concert D Minor

1. Minor Fives – Quarter Notes

2. Minor Fives – Eighth Notes

3. Thirds

4. Expanding Intervals

5. Percussion Feature
Houston: Are You Really There?

Listen and watch carefully as the percussion section plays.

6. Follow the Leader

Concert B♭ Major

1. Major Fives – Quarter Notes

2. Major Fives – Eighth Notes

3. Thirds

4. Expanding Intervals

5. Percussion Feature
Traveling at Warp Speed

Listen and watch carefully as the percussion section plays.

6. Follow the Leader

BB203TSX

Concert G Minor

1. Minor Fives – Quarter Notes

2. Minor Fives – Eighth Notes

3. Thirds

4. Expanding Intervals

5. Percussion Feature
The Suspense Builds

Listen and watch carefully as the percussion section plays.

6. Follow the Leader

solo/soli   band   solo/soli   band

solo/soli   band   all

Concert E♭ Major

1. Major Fives – Quarter Notes

2. Major Fives – Eighth Notes

3. Thirds

4. Expanding Intervals

5. Percussion Feature
Turbulence

Listen and watch carefully as the percussion section plays.

6. Follow the Leader

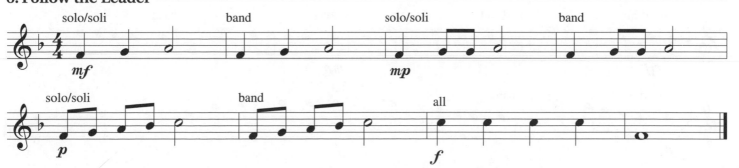

BB203TSX

Concert C Minor

1. Minor Fives – Quarter Notes

2. Minor Fives – Eighth Notes

3. Thirds

4. Expanding Intervals

5. Percussion Feature
Sounds of Home

Listen and watch carefully as the percussion section plays.

6. Follow the Leader

solo/soli · band · solo/soli · band

solo/soli · band · all

Concert A♭ Major

1. Major Fives – Quarter Notes

2. Major Fives – Eighth Notes

3. Thirds

4. Expanding Intervals

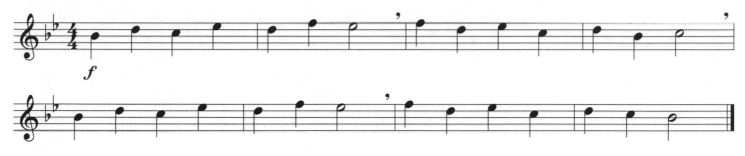

5. Percussion Feature
Touchdown!   Listen and watch carefully as the percussion section plays.

6. Follow the Leader

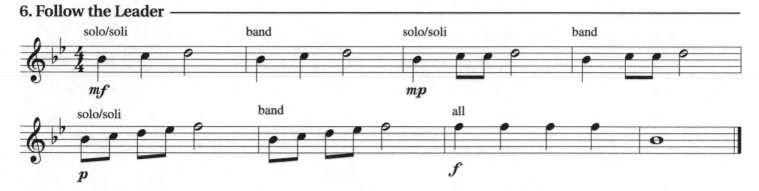

BB203TSX

Concert F Minor

1. Minor Fives – Quarter Notes

2. Minor Fives – Eighth Notes

3. Thirds

4. Expanding Intervals

5. Percussion Feature
  A Landing Celebration

Listen and watch carefully as the percussion section plays.

6. Follow the Leader

Part 2 – Advanced Warm-ups

In this section, you will review the keys from Part 1 while learning some new concepts presented in the following format:

1. Major/Harmonic Minor Scales and Arpeggios (quarter notes) – In Part 1, you focused on the first five notes of each scale. In Part 2, you will work on the entire scale, followed by an arpeggio that now reaches to the top of the scale before descending (1 – 3 – 5 – 8 – 5 – 3 – 1).

2. Major/Harmonic Minor Scales and Arpeggios (eighth notes) – This is the same exercise as No. 1 using eighth notes instead of quarter notes.

3. Major/Harmonic Minor Chords – The first thing you will notice in this exercise is the pyramid icon. The pyramid reminds you to listen carefully and pay close attention to balance. Go to page 33 to learn more about ensemble balance using the Balance Pyramid. There is a fermata at the end of these chord progressions. Notice the Roman numerals in this exercise; these indicate the kind of chord that you will hear.

4. Thirds – This exercise is similar to the Thirds exercise in Part 1 but uses eighth notes instead of quarter notes.

5. Percussion Feature.

6. Chromatic Pivot Scale – This exercise is similar to the Expanding Intervals exercise in Part 1 but uses only descending chromatic notes. You should review the sharps and flats needed for this exercise before you play (see accidentals in the Glossary on page 33).

7. Chromatic Scale – These scales go up and down using half steps. Because a key signature is not necessary to play each scale, you will see the following reminder: No key signature! Review the accidentals in your scale and consult your fingering chart if needed. You may also need to look at the Glossary section on enharmonics (page 34).

8. Chorale – Notice the pyramid again. Remember to listen carefully and adjust for balance and blend. The chorales in this section will be in different styles. Look for the style or tempo term at the beginning of each piece, review the definition, and watch your director who will give you conducting gestures that will communicate style.

Concert C Major

1. Major Scale and Arpeggio – Quarter Notes

scale

arpeggio

mf

2. Major Scale and Arpeggio – Eighth Notes

scale

arpeggio

mp

3. Major Chords

Listen to the direction of the moving bass part.

f I   IV   V   I   I   V   V   I

4. Thirds

p

5. Percussion Feature

Moon March

Listen and watch carefully as the percussion section plays.

mf   *p*   *mf*   *p*   *ff*

6. Chromatic Pivot Scale

p   *f*   *p*

7. Chromatic Scale

No key signature!

mf

8. Chorale

St. Anne
William Croft, 1708

Giocoso (♩ = 132)

f

Concert A Minor

1. Harmonic Minor Scale and Arpeggio – Quarter Notes

2. Harmonic Minor Scale and Arpeggio – Eighth Notes

3. Minor Chords

Listen to the direction of the moving bass part.

4. Thirds

5. Percussion Feature
Weightlessness

Listen and watch carefully as the percussion section plays.

6. Chromatic Pivot Scale

7. Chromatic Scale

No key signature!

8. Chorale

Wer nur den lieben Gott
Georg Neumark, 1640

Andante sostenuto

BB203TSX

Concert F Major

1. Major Scale and Arpeggio – Quarter Notes

2. Major Scale and Arpeggio – Eighth Notes

3. Major Chords

4. Thirds

5. Percussion Feature
Rocket Renegade

Listen and watch carefully as the percussion section plays.

6. Chromatic Pivot Scale

7. Chromatic Scale
No key signature!

8. Chorale

Wem in Leidenstagen
Friederich Filitz, 1847

Andantino

Concert D Minor

1. Harmonic Minor Scale and Arpeggio – Quarter Notes

2. Harmonic Minor Scale and Arpeggio – Eighth Notes

3. Minor Chord

Listen to the direction of the moving bass part.

4. Thirds

5. Percussion Feature
An Argument: What To Do Next?

Listen and watch carefully as the percussion section plays.

6. Chromatic Pivot Scale

7. Chromatic Scale

No key signature!

8. Chorale

St. Cross
John B. Dykes, 1861

Adagio

BB203TSX

Concert B♭ Major

1. Major Scale and Arpeggio – Quarter Notes

scale

, arpeggio

mf

2. Major Scale and Arpeggio – Eighth Notes

scale

arpeggio

mp

3. Major Chords

Listen to the direction of the moving bass part.

f   I   IV   V   I   I   V   V   I

4. Thirds

p

5. Percussion Feature

Dodging the Meteors

Listen and watch carefully as the percussion section plays.

f ———————— p < f ———————— p < f

6. Chromatic Pivot Scale

p ———————— f   ———————— p

7. Chromatic Scale

No key signature!

mf

8. Chorale

Voller Wunder
Johann G. Eberling, 1666

Moderato

mf   mp   mf

mp   mf ———————— f

rit.

Concert G Minor

Concert E♭ Major

1. Major Scale and Arpeggio – Quarter Notes

scale   arpeggio

mf

2. Major Scale and Arpeggio – Eighth Notes

scale   arpeggio

mp

3. Major Chords

Listen to the direction of the moving bass part.

f   I   IV   V   I   I   V   V   I

4. Thirds

p

5. Percussion Feature
There and Back

Listen and watch carefully as the percussion section plays.

p   *f*   *p*

6. Chromatic Pivot Scale

p   *f*   *p*

7. Chromatic Scale

No key signature!

mf

8. Chorale

St. Crispin
George J. Elvey, 1862

Cantabile (♩ = 116)

mp   *mf*

p   *f*   *p*

Concert C Minor

1. Harmonic Minor Scale and Arpeggio – Quarter Notes

2. Harmonic Minor Scale and Arpeggio – Eighth Notes

3. Minor Chords

Listen to the direction of the moving bass part.

4. Thirds

5. Percussion Feature
Finding What We Came For

Listen and watch carefully as the percussion section plays.

6. Chromatic Pivot Scale

7. Chromatic Scale
No key signature!

8. Chorale

Sieh, hier bin ich
"Geistreiches Gesangbuch," Darmstadt, 1698

Andante espressivo

rit.

BB203TSX

Concert A♭ Major

1. Major Scale and Arpeggio – Quarter Notes

2. Major Scale and Arpeggio – Eighth Notes

3. Major Chords

Listen to the direction of the moving bass part.

4. Thirds

5. Percussion Feature
We're Coming Home!

Listen and watch carefully as the percussion section plays.

6. Chromatic Pivot Scale

7. Chromatic Scale

No key signature!

8. Chorale

Dunstan
Joseph Barnby, 1883

Allegretto

Concert F Minor

1. Harmonic Minor Scale and Arpeggio – Quarter Notes

2. Harmonic Minor Scale and Arpeggio – Eighth Notes

3. Minor Chords

Listen to the direction of the moving bass part.

i   iv   V   i   i   V   V   i

4. Thirds

5. Percussion Feature
Family and Friends Greet Us!

Listen and watch carefully as the percussion section plays.

6. Chromatic Pivot Scale

7. Chromatic Scale

No key signature!

8. Chorale

Southwell
"Psalter," William Daman, 1579

Grave

Part 3 – Key Change Studies

Composers often write music that changes key from the first key used. In this section you will practice performing and listening to key changes. You will see asterisks (*) throughout. Each asterisk indicates the note that is altered by the key change. It is a reminder to change the note according to the new key signature. With practice, you will not need the asterisk; just look at the key signature. This section takes you through five major keys. Challenge yourself to try the scale patterns and familiar songs in different keys.

Part 3 is presented in the following format:

1. Major Fives – As in Part 1, this exercise moves up and down the first five notes of each scale, but the arpeggio is omitted. In addition, this exercise moves from the first key (first three measures) to the next related key (next three measures). The related key will always be an interval of a fourth away from the original key. For example, the first key presented is concert C. A perfect fourth from concert C is concert F and that will be your new key. Listen to how the interval sounds. Notes a fourth away from each other have a close musical relationship.

2. Major Scales – Full scale patterns return in this exercise. They begin in one key and move to the related key. Remember to check the new key signature located after the double bar.

3. Familiar Pieces – There are several pieces in this section that you will recognize. Play each melody in the original key, then check your key signature as the melody is repeated in the new key.

4. More Familiar Pieces – This exercise is similar to No. 3 except that the pieces are longer and utilize a broader range of notes.

Concert C to F Major

1. Major Fives

2. Major Scales

3. Hot Cross Buns
English Folk Song

4. Skip to My Lou
American Folk Song

*note altered by key change

Concert F to B♭ Major

1. Major Fives

2. Major Scales

3. Jim Along Josie

American Folk Song

4. Mister Banjo

Creole Folk Song

*note altered by key change

BB203TSX

Concert B♭ to E♭ Major

1. Major Fives

2. Major Scales

3. Au claire de la lune

French Folk Song

4. Ode to Joy

Ludwig van Beethoven

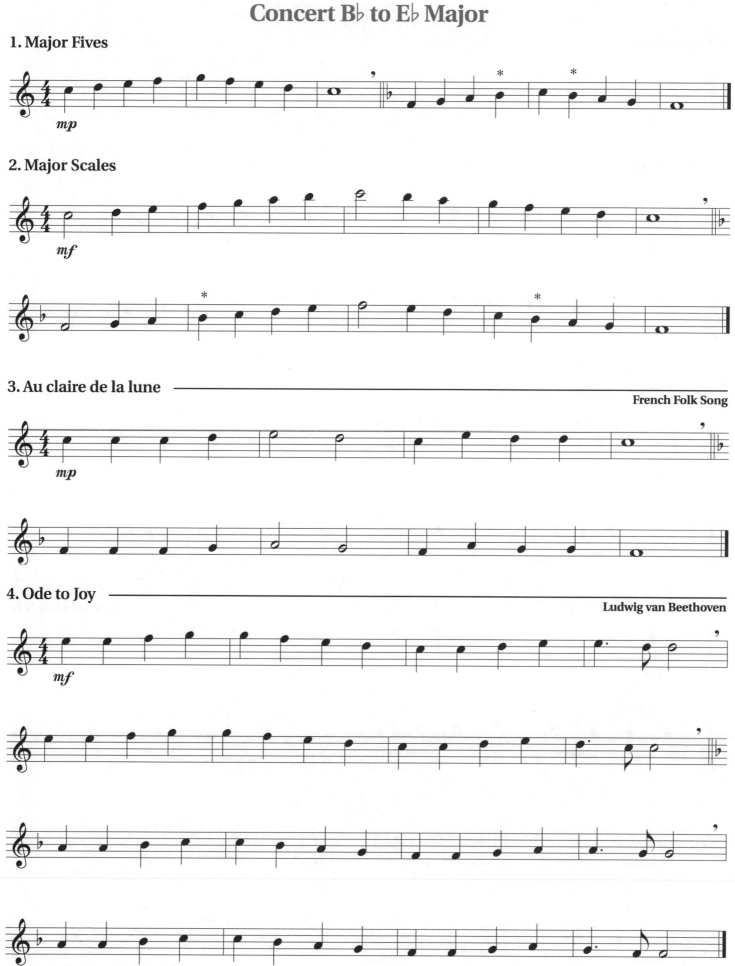

*note altered by key change

Concert E♭ to A♭ Major

1. Major Fives

2. Major Scales

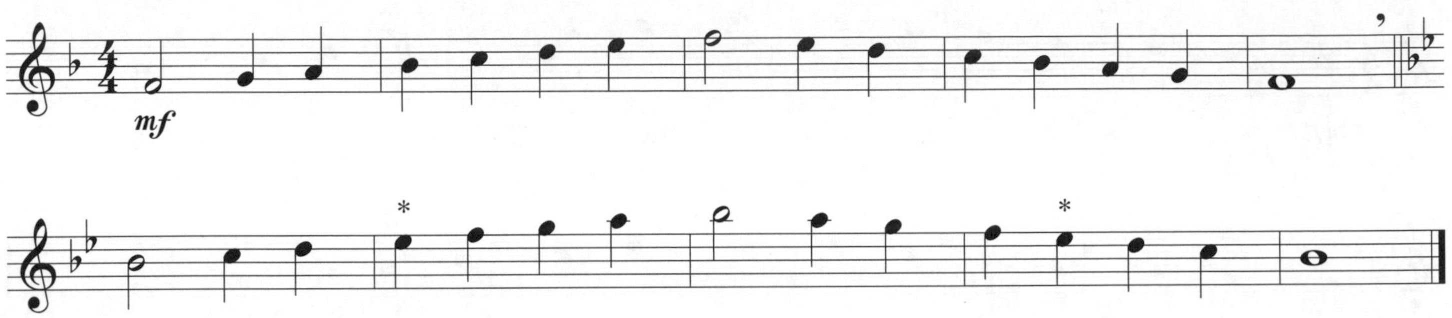

3. Musette

Johann Sebastian Bach

4. Yankee Doodle

American Folk Song

*note altered by key change

Part 4 – Articulation Studies

Articulations indicate how notes are to be tongued and released. Each piece has a different articulation challenge. Some will focus on one main articulation and others will ask you to perform different articulations in the same piece. Your director will show differences in articulation through different conducting gestures.

Plain Note – The plain note receives full value. Tongue the plain note with precision and end it with an open release.

Tenuto Note – The tenuto note receives full value. Tongue the tenuto note gently and play tenuto phrases with a continuous stream of air. Repeated tenuto notes express a smooth *(legato)*, horizontal style.

Staccato Note – The staccato note is shortened in value. Tongue the staccato note with precision and end it with an open release. Repeated staccato notes sound detached.

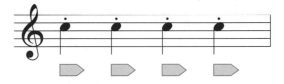

Accented Note – The accented note has weight. Tongue the accented note with confidence, using air to create emphasis. End the accented note with an open release. Repeated accented notes are separated with space.

Marcato Note – The marcato note is forceful yet shortened in value. Tongue the marcato note with confidence and end it with an open release. Marcato notes are shorter than accented notes.

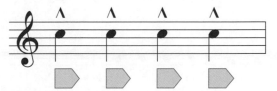

Slurred Notes – Slurred notes are smooth and connected. Tongue only the first note in each group of slurred notes.

Articulation Studies

1. Are You Slurring?

2. Déjà vu

3. Are You Tonguing?

4. Said with an Accent

5. Dots and Dashes

Articulation Studies

6. Déjà vu Again

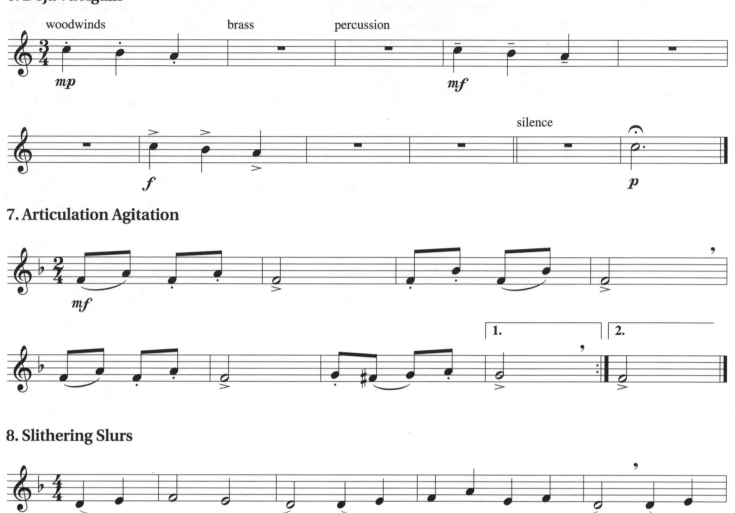

7. Articulation Agitation

8. Slithering Slurs

9. Twisted Tonguing

10. Lotsa Dotsa

Part 5 – Flexibility Studies

Composers often write music that requires you to play a wide range of notes for a long period of time. The following exercises will help you to improve your tone, range, and endurance. As you practice each group of intervals, focus on good breath support and smooth slurs.

Glossary

A glossary is a mini-dictionary. In it you will find information about musical terms, symbols, signs, and performance techniques. All of the information in the glossary relates to the skills needed to develop outstanding musicianship.

Accidentals: Accidentals are sharps, flats, or naturals placed in front of notes. They remain "powerful" for an entire measure.

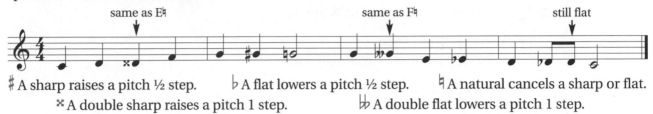

♯ A sharp raises a pitch ½ step.   ♭ A flat lowers a pitch ½ step.   ♮ A natural cancels a sharp or flat.

✕ A double sharp raises a pitch 1 step.   ♭♭ A double flat lowers a pitch 1 step.

Balance: A band sound is balanced when each part can be heard in proper relationship to all parts. A very famous band leader named W. Francis McBeth diagramed a balanced band sound in the shape of a pyramid.

Balance Pyramid: The Balance Pyramid will help your band develop a warm, dark sound. Like the pyramids of Egypt, a balanced band sound must have a sturdy foundation. Use the Balance Pyramid each time you see the pyramid icon in this book.

= use the Balance Pyramid

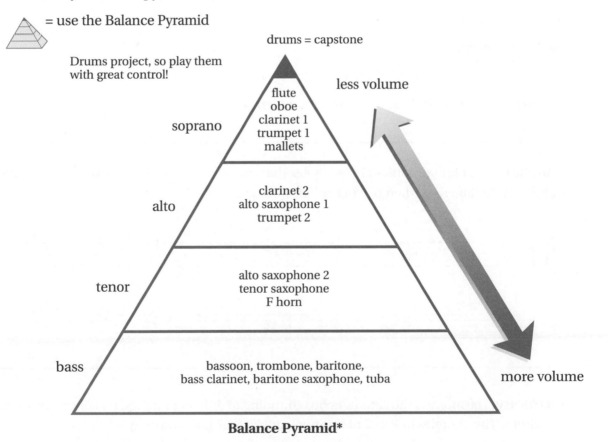

Balance Pyramid*

Incorrect Balance: A band sound is imbalanced when each part cannot be heard in proper relationship to all parts. An imbalanced band sound can be represented by an altered pyramid.

too much high   too much high

not enough low   not enough middle   not enough low

*Taken from "Effective Performance of Band Music" by W. Francis McBeth, published by Southern Music.

Chorale: A lyrical hymn often utilizing four-part harmony (see the Balance Pyramid above).

Dynamics: Dynamics indicate volume levels. Dynamics can change, remain steady, or bring about surprise.

Changing Dynamics

crescendo (cresc.) – gradually louder

decrescendo (decresc.) or
diminuendo (dim.) – gradually softer

poco a poco – little by little

Steady Dynamics

pp   *pianissimo* – very soft

p   *piano* – soft

mp   *mezzo piano* – medium soft

mf   *mezzo forte* – medium loud

f   *forte* – loud

ff   *fortissimo* – very loud

Surprise Dynamics

fp   *forte-piano* – loud, then immediately soft

sf or *sfz*   *sforzando* or *sforzato* – a strong, sudden accent

---

Enharmonics: Enharmonics are two notes that sound the same but are written differently. Use the same fingering when playing enharmonics.

Harmony: Harmony is the simultaneous sounding of different pitches, usually in the form of a chord. The chorales in Part 2 of this book utilize four-part harmony.

Intonation: Intonation is the measure of your ability to match correct pitch. Good intonation is a result of careful listening, correct embouchure formation, and proper breath support.

Key Signatures: Key signatures are the flats or sharps found at the beginning of each staff. They show which notes are altered in a piece and indicate either a major or minor tonality.

Order of Flats and Sharps: Flats or sharps appear in the key signature from left to right. Reverse the order of flats to get the order of sharps.

Relative Key Signatures: Major and minor key signatures that are the same are called relative key signatures. Because A minor shares the same key signature with C major, these two keys are related. Relative key signatures are explored in Part 1 and Part 2 of this book.

Parallel Key Signatures: Parallel major and minor keys share the same tonic note (home tone), but not the same key signature. Add three flats to any major key signature to produce its parallel minor key signature. Remember: flats cancel sharps.

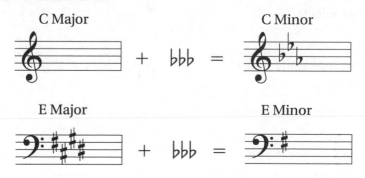

Melody: Melody is a succession of musical tones. Unlike harmony, which is vertical, melody is linear or horizontal. For melody to have meaning, its pitches must have rhythmic value.

Pause Markings: These markings interrupt or suspend the flow of the music.

Common Pause Markings

//   *caesura* – a short pause

⌢   *fermata* – lengthen the note or rest

G.P. (grand pause) – a long pause

Pitch: Pitch is the highness or lowness of a tone. In music, pitches are named according to the musical alphabet. The musical alphabet consists of seven repeating letters: A, B, C, D, E, F, G.

Repeat Signs: Repeat signs provide direction and often "map out" the form of a piece.

Common Repeat Signs

Coda – the concluding section or passage

D.C. al Coda – go back to the beginning and play to the Coda sign ⊕, then skip to the Coda

D.C. al fine – go back to the beginning and play to the end, indicated by *fine*

D.S. al Coda – go back to the sign 𝄋, play to the Coda sign ⊕, then skip to the Coda

D.S. al fine – go back to the sign 𝄋 and play to the end, indicated by *fine*

fine – the end (The Italian word *fine* is pronounced FEE-nay.)

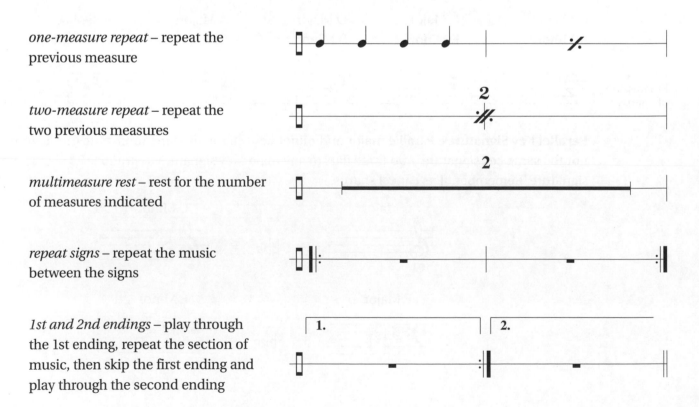

one-measure repeat – repeat the previous measure

two-measure repeat – repeat the two previous measures

multimeasure rest – rest for the number of measures indicated

repeat signs – repeat the music between the signs

1st and 2nd endings – play through the 1st ending, repeat the section of music, then skip the first ending and play through the second ending

Rhythm: Rhythm is musical movement in time. While the beat is the steady pulse of the music, rhythm involves the placement and duration of notes.

Rhythmic Groupings: Notes are grouped together by beams. Typically, the rhythmic value of each beamed grouping equals one beat.

Scales: Scales are sequences of notes that ascend and descend by specific intervals. All scales in this book move by step.

Major and Minor Scales: Major and minor scales are constructed with eight scale tones (diatonic steps). Minor scales are unique because they appear in three different forms: natural, harmonic, and melodic. Part 2 of this book explores major and harmonic minor keys and scales.

Chromatic Scale: The chromatic scale is constructed with semitones (half steps). It is an important scale to memorize because it contains every note playable on your instrument. This scale is also explored in Part 2 of this book.

Style Terms: Style terms are used to describe an intended mood. They often appear along with tempo terms at the beginning of a piece or at a new section within a piece.

Common Style Terms

animato – animated

agitato – agitated

cantabile – in a singing style

dolce – sweetly

espressivo – expressively

giocoso – joyfully

grandioso – in a grand style

grazioso – gracefully

leggiero – lightly

maestoso – majestically

marziale – in a martial style

pesante – in a heavy style

scherzando – in a playful style

secco – very short and dry

sostenuto – sustained

Tempo Terms: Tempo terms indicate the speed of the beat. Tempo can remain steady or it can change to make a piece more interesting.

Steady Tempo Terms

grave – very slow and solemn

largo – very slow ($\quarternote = 40–60$)

larghetto – a little faster than largo ($\quarternote = 60–66$)

adagio – slow ($\quarternote = 66–76$)

andante – moderately slow, at a walking pace ($\quarternote = 76–108$)

andantino – a little faster than andante

moderato – moderate ($\quarternote = 108–120$)

allegretto – a little slower than allegro

allegro – fast, cheerful ($\quarternote = 120–168$)

vivace – fast, vivacious

presto – very fast ($\quarternote = 168–200$)

prestissimo – as fast as possible ($\quarternote = 200+$)

Increasing Tempo Terms

accelerando (accel.) – gradually faster
stringendo (string.) – gradually faster, usually with a crescendo
doppio moviment – twice as fast
più mosso – more motion, faster
con moto – with motion, keep the tempo moving

Decreasing Tempo Terms

rallentando (rall.) – gradually slower
ritardando (rit.) – gradually slower
ritenuto – immediate reduction in speed
allargando (allarg.) – gradually slower and broader
morendo – gradually slower and softer, fading
calando – gradually slower and softer
smorzando (smorz.) – gradually slower and softer
meno mosso – less motion, slower

Miscellaneous Tempo Terms

l'istesso tempo – keep the same tempo
a tempo – resume previous tempo (after *rit.*)
tempo primo – return to the first tempo
rubato – flexible, elastic tempo

Timbre [tam-ber]: Timbre is tone color. When two or more different instruments play the same pitch, timbre is the element that makes it possible to tell them apart.

Instrument Timbre: To achieve a desirable sound on your instrument, use correct embouchure formation and proper breath support. Percussionists should use correct stick grip and proper stick height.

Time Signatures: Time signatures are two numbers placed at the beginning of a composition to indicate its meter. The top number indicates the number of beats per measure and the bottom number indicates the unit of beat (4 for quarter note, 2 for half note, 8 for eighth note).

Familiar Time Signatures

Tuning: Tuning is the matching of correct pitch.

The Science Behind Tuning: When you play your instrument, invisible sound waves travel through the air. When two or more instruments are in tune, their sound waves match. When two or more instruments are not in tune, their sound waves do not match.

in tune – stable sound   *not in tune* – unstable sound

Flat Versus Sharp: A pitch that is too low is flat. A pitch that is too high is sharp. Use your ear to determine if a pitch is flat or sharp.

Using Your Ear: Your ear reveals the accuracy of your tuning note. When your note is in tune, it will match the reference pitch and sound stable. If your note sounds unstable, it is not in tune.

Using Good Technique: Correct embouchure formation and proper breath support are key to playing in tune. Adjusting your instrument may also be necessary.

Adjusting Your Instrument: Your band director will show you which part of your instrument to adjust. If your tuning note is flat, adjust by pushing in. If your tuning note is sharp, adjust by pulling out.

Tuning the Band: Ensemble tuning requires careful listening, patience, and plenty of practice.

Vertical Tuning: Vertical tuning works from bottom to top. In vertical tuning, the tubas tune using an electronic tuner. Follow these steps:

1. Listen carefully as the tuba section holds the reference pitch.

2. Add tuning notes one section at a time, working up the Balance Pyramid.

3. Adjust instruments if necessary.

4. Repeat steps 1–3 until the band sound is uniform.

Horizontal Tuning: Horizontal tuning works across the woodwinds and brasses. In horizontal tuning, the principal clarinet and principal trumpet tune using an electronic tuner. Follow these steps:

For the woodwind family…

1. Listen carefully as the principal clarinet holds the reference pitch.

2. Add principal players from all woodwind sections, adjusting instruments if necessary.

3. Add all woodwind players, adjusting instruments if necessary.

4. Repeat steps 1–3 until the woodwind sound is uniform.

For the brass family…

1. Listen carefully as the principal trumpet holds the reference pitch.

2. Add principal players from all brass sections, adjusting instruments if necessary.

3. Add all brass players, adjusting instruments if necessary.

4. Repeat steps 1–3 until the brass sound is uniform.

Tuning Individually: Individual tuning requires careful listening and the use of an electronic tuner.

Using an Electronic Tuner: An electronic tuner displays the accuracy of your tuning note. When your note is flat, the tuning gauge points left. When your note is sharp, the tuning gauge points right. When your note is in tune, the tuning gauge points dead center. Follow these steps:

1. Play your tuning note and hold it steady.

2. Watch the tuning gauge to see if your tuning note is flat or sharp.

3. Adjust your instrument if necessary.

4. Repeat steps 1–3 until the gauge points dead center.

Tuning a Section: Sectional tuning requires careful listening, patience, and plenty of practice. Section members should use horizontal tuning, guiding off the principal player. Section members can also tune using an electronic tuner.

Appendices

An appendix is a section at the end of a book that contains extra material. The following is a list of what you will be able to find:

Basic Chromatic Scale

Advanced Chromatic Scale

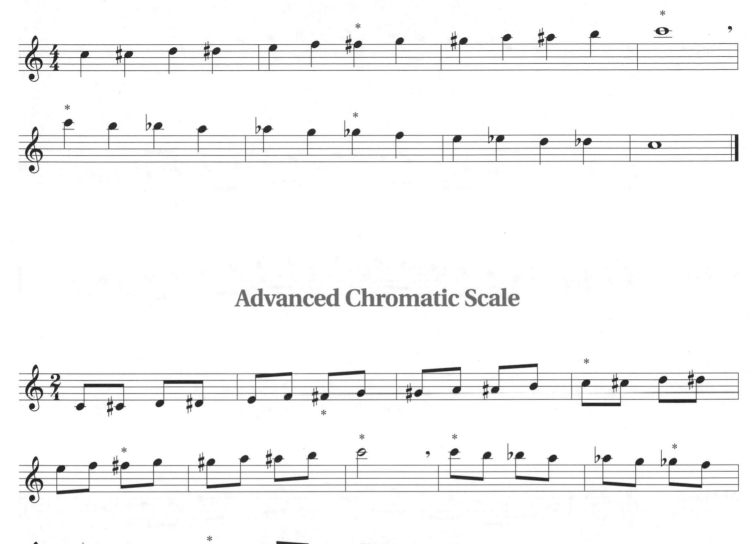

*use alternate fingering

Tuning Notes

Traditional Band Tuning Note = Concert B♭	Recommended Tuning Note	Adjustment Procedure
		adjust mouthpiece

Major Flat Scales
1 Octave

C Major
Concert B♭

F Major
Concert E♭

B♭ Major
Concert A♭

E♭ Major
Concert D♭

A♭ Major
Concert G♭

D♭ Major
Concert B

G♭ Major
Concert E

C♭ Major
Concert A

Order of Flats
B♭, E♭, A♭, D♭, G♭, C♭, F♭

Major Sharp Scales
1 Octave

C Major
Concert B♭

G Major
Concert F

D Major
Concert C

A Major
Concert G

E Major
Concert D

B Major
Concert A

F♯ Major
Concert E

C♯ Major
Concert B

Order of Sharps
F♯, C♯, G♯, D♯, A♯, E♯, B♯

Natural Minor Flat Scales
1 Octave

A Minor
Concert G

D Minor
Concert C

G Minor
Concert F

C Minor
Concert Bb

F Minor
Concert Eb

Bb Minor
Concert Ab

Eb Minor
Concert Db

Ab Minor
Concert Gb

Order of Flats
Bb, Eb, Ab, Db, Gb, Cb, Fb

Natural Minor Sharp Scales
1 Octave

Order of Sharps
F♯, C♯, G♯, D♯, A♯, E♯, B♯

Harmonic Minor Flat Scales
1 Octave

A Minor
Concert G

D Minor
Concert C

G Minor
Concert F

C Minor
Concert B♭

F Minor
Concert E♭

B♭ Minor
Concert A♭

E♭ Minor
Concert D♭

A♭ Minor
Concert G♭

Order of Flats
B♭, E♭, A♭, D♭, G♭, C♭, F♭

Harmonic Minor Sharp Scales
1 Octave

Order of Sharps
F♯, C♯, G♯, D♯, A♯, E♯, B♯